Choose to Just Be

Choose to Just Be

The 4 Steps to an Easier Life

Michell Torres, LCSW

Contents:

Introduction:

Stop Struggling

When you look back at your life, do you see it as a journey or do you feel like it's been mostly an uphill hike?
What if you could stop struggling and allow your path to be easy?

I have been a psychotherapist for over 25 years. Most of my professional career has been working in medical hospitals doing psychiatric crisis work. I was a manager at two hospitals for more than half of my career and was often sought out for my expertise and training. In addition to working for a hospital, I have also had a private practice for the past 20 years. Daily, colleagues turned to me for consultation about how to assist the patients we were treating. By many, I am considered an expert in my field. I had a solid career with a good company, doing work at which I excelled. And...I walked away from all of it.

I've worked with thousands of clients through both private practice and at the hospitals. Most of the time, people begin working with a therapist because they have a problem and they are looking for direction on how to solve it. They feel they have a decision to make and they don't know what to do. Many are looking for a change in their circumstances.

A few years ago, I came to a crossroads in my own life. On the outside, my life was going well, but I wasn't happy. I needed a change, a different direction. I loved the work I was doing, but the job was no longer the right fit for me. And I knew it wasn't about getting the same job at a different company. I needed to figure out how to get to the life that I really wanted to be living. The truth was, the place I was at in my life and where my soul wanted to be were two different places.

I wasn't living an emotionally fulfilled life. In fact, it wasn't the life I knew I was destined to live. But I was stuck because I did not know how to make the changes I wanted.

Do you sometimes feel like you are waiting to start your REAL life?
...the life you were actually meant to be living

My own experiences and my work with others led to the *Choose to Just Be* system. The entire program is outlined in this book. You will see real changes when you apply this program to your life. It has been a game changer for both me and my clients.

It's based on a simple concept; however, implementing it into your life could take some practice. Do not fear. I have all the help you will need.

Start by going to www.ChooseToJustBe.com. Then join me and I will walk you through the online programs where you will gain more understanding and receive individual assistance for your specific questions and problems.

Before we get further into the book, I want to say a quick word about faith and spirituality. It's a big part of this program, and there are many different descriptions that people have for the power that is greater than all of us. In an effort to be as inclusive as possible, I will describe that power as both God and the universe, interchangeably. The true focus of this system is not on how you describe that power. It's about how you connect to it. Go ahead and use whatever word or description works best for you.

1

Let Go and Allow Easy

Our culture defines success by the outcomes we produce: a bigger car, a nicer house, better vacations, and the perfect looking family. We are taught that the way to obtain this success is to try harder, work more, and dig deeper. We chase after this dream because of a desire to experience happiness and a feeling of security in our lives. And, even if we achieve the financial success and emotional security we are seeking, we don't get to stop the effort. We have to continue working to keep what we have.

This transformational system will show you that the endless pursuit of peace, happiness, and security doesn't result in any of those. It is through the letting go of trying to reach your goals under your own power where you will learn that trying harder is not the power move. Letting go is. By allowing a power greater than yourself to do the heavy lifting, you can settle into your life and begin achieving your dreams with less effort.

In my own life, I realized that all my hard work and struggling was not getting me the contentment that I was seeking. I also discovered that it's not an easy thing to just "let go." What I developed through this process was not merely a better problem-solving technique, but an entirely new approach to life.

When faced with a decision about whether or not to change careers, I did what most of us would do. I turned to self-help books, mentors, coaches, and friends and family. I got a lot of good advice, probably a lot of the same advice that you have gotten in your life. I was directed both to make a logical decision and to listen to my heart. A few even said that I will just know intuitively what to do.

More than one person told me to take out a piece of paper and make a list of the pros and cons of staying at my current job. Whatever list had more on it was the choice to make. Doing that, however, did not make me feel confident that I had the right decision. As much as this advice was helpful, I was still left with one big question about my career:

What is the best decision for me?

I was struggling because I did not know what to do. Either option of staying or leaving my job had its benefits and drawbacks. My situation was probably not that much different than yours. You might be having difficulties in a relationship or in your job.

You might be having financial problems or health problems. Do you have questions similar to the ones that I had for myself?

Do you know how to get where you want to go in life?
Do you know what decisions you should be making to reach your goals?
Do you know which choices are the best ones for you?

You might know what your goal is. But do you know how to get there? What I found when I was in search of direction was a lot of the same information. And, in reality, it wasn't really helping me very much. It sounded good. It was good advice. But it wasn't helping me achieve my dreams.

My own struggle led to a life-changing way of "doing life." This system is an approach to problems that I had never tried before, even though I thought I had. You see, the information wasn't new. In fact, the information has been around a long time, but I did not know how to apply it. **And because I wasn't applying it correctly, it wasn't working.** It was not about being lazy or unmotivated. It wasn't working because I was focusing on changing those situations outside of myself (my job, my relationships, my finances, etc.) instead of changing my approach to those problems. I also did not know how to get over the hurdles that inevitably came up.

This isn't one more book or one more program that focuses on self-help. In fact, it's not about helping yourself at all. It's about letting go and using the power in the universe to provide solutions. It's a way of living that shows you how to stop struggling and allow yourself the life you always knew you were supposed to live.

As you sail along on this journey we call life and point your ship in the direction you want to go, you will find that powers greater than you may appear to steer you off course. Strong winds, ocean currents and storms seem to be keeping you from your goals. You can use your own strength to try and sail in the direction of your choice, fighting against the waves and struggling to stay afloat. Or you can allow the wind and currents to guide you, with faith that those powers are pointing you toward the destination where your soul longs to be.

You may be asking at this point, "What do I have to do?" "What steps do I have to take?" "How much work am I going to have to do?" Actually, you don't have to do more work at all.

Just let go and allow easy.

2

Just Be

Here is the program summed up in four steps:

1. Be Open
2. Be Bold
3. Be Still
4. Be Aware

That's it. It's that easy. The concept is short and sweet. It really only consists of eight words. And those eight words can change your life. Yes, the concept is simple. But, it's learning how to give up your need for control and allow a power greater than yourself to guide you that could take a little bit of practice on your part.

The ego and your rational "thinking brain" will want to run the show. This is the part where you "choose to" take these four steps and change the direction of your life.

Take a look at this simple example of a day where a client of mine was late leaving her house on her way to a morning meeting at her job. It took less than two minutes to do, and it added no time or energy to her day because she was driving her car while implementing the steps.

1. **Be Open:** She does not deny that she is running late to work. She accepts her current situation without trying to fix it. She is not judging herself or berating herself for being late.

2. **Be Bold:** She asks God, or the universe, to help her get to work on time and expects that help will be provided. Then, she lets go of trying to control the situation. She allows all possible solutions.

3. **Be Still:** Now she waits on God to help her out. She is not stressed, upset, or worried. She has asked for help and is confident that she will receive it. She stops any of her own attempts to control the situation.

4. **Be Aware:** After asking for help, she begins looking for the solution and how it will be provided for her. *(The solution may come in the form of an open parking space near the front of the building; it may be in a canceled or delayed morning meeting, or she may be late to work and the outcome of that situation becomes a stepping stone to another solution, etc.)*

Regardless of the outcome of her arrival at work, she will have been provided the best solution.

The rest of this book will explain how to utilize each step and have those experiences where you are not anxious or stressed and are confident that you will get help. Don't worry if all of this does not make complete sense yet. It will become much clearer in the upcoming chapters.

You have probably heard the concept to "just be" or "let it be." There are bumper stickers and famous songs that have these phrases, and many books have been written on the subject. Why is that such an important point? So many of us are struggling just to get through the day. We're really trying so hard, but just don't feel like we're succeeding at this thing called life. If someone said to you, "just be," you may not really know how to do that or it wouldn't feel like it made much sense to you.

Dogs are a good example of "just being." They don't usually spend a lot of time worrying or struggling. They don't care about what they look like or whether they are well liked. They go about doing what feels good to them, and they enjoy being dogs. They don't apologize for their personality or their looks. And I doubt that they are ashamed of who they are, even when they don't follow the rules that we want them to follow, like staying out of the trash. They are still just being dogs.

The same analogy can be applied when looking at ourselves when we were young, long before we learned to attach all of those other expectations to our behavior. Toddlers are a great example. Take a look at a two-year-old or think back to when you were that age. Do toddlers judge themselves for their appearance? Do they focus on what they "should be" doing or what others will think of them? Or do they spend their energy on what they like and what they want to do? **Just be who you are**. That's one part of this program.

You are exactly who you are supposed to be.

The other part of "just being" is to stop trying to be in charge of the universe. Let go of trying to run this big world all by yourself and allow the power that is greater than you to continue being greater than you. Once you do that, you can focus on just being who you are.

You can use the steps in this program when faced with a problem or a decision that you need to make in your life. But you will quickly find it's much more than a problem-solving technique.

So, is this a book about decision making, spirituality, or how to approach life differently so that you can achieve your dreams?

Scientists estimate that we have about 60,000 thoughts in our head each day. One category of those thoughts is about trying to figure things out. We spend a lot of time and energy trying to decide which choice to make about situations in our lives:

- *What do I do about this person in my life?*
- *How do I fix that situation?*
- *Should I stay where I'm at or look for something better?*

Another category of our thoughts is about wanting things in our life to be different:

- *I wish I had more money.*
- *Why can't my (friend, partner, husband, wife, child, parent, coworker) just act differently?*
- *I wish I were taller, shorter, thinner, prettier.*
- *It's too hot today. I want it to cool down.*
- *It's too cold today. I want it warm up.*

A third category for our thoughts is our own judgment. See if you can catch yourself in your own internal dialogue and look at how much you're judging others and judging yourself.

- *That person is pretty.* Or, *That person is ugly.*
- *He drives like a maniac.*
- *Did you really just try to bring 15 items to the 10 items or less line?*
- *I just can't make good decisions.*
- *I am so stupid! Why did I do that?*

We often think that our decisions and actions only come from the part of the brain that uses logic and reasoning. Yet most of our brain's resources are devoted to the subconscious processes. Neuroscientists indicate that 85-95% of our brain's cognitive activities are subconscious. In addition, noted cell biologist, Dr. Bruce Lipton, explains that "the subconscious mind processes some 20 million environmental stimuli per second verses forty environmental stimuli by the conscious mind in the same second."

Instead of keeping our attention on our conscious reasoning when making decisions, let's become aware of what the rest of the mind is engaged in. All of those thoughts in your head about decisions, desires and judgements? Well, they aren't helping you to find the happiness and contentment that you are truly seeking. The *Just Be* system can help you get out of your "thinking brain" when facing choices and engage your subconscious mind while connecting to a power greater than yourself, thereby allowing you to struggle less.

If you are struggling less, are more content, and less fearful...do you think that could help you to achieve the life that you know you are supposed to be living? Some of the common difficulties that so many of us share are that we feel alone, unsupported, lost and discontented. Connecting with a power or an energy that unites us all can help with all of those feelings.

So, is this a book about decision making, spirituality, or how to approach life differently? Yes, it is!

3

The Four Steps

Here is the outline for the program.

- **Step 1: BE OPEN:** Accept and agree with your situation, including your feelings about the situation. Stop trying to change your current circumstances.
- **Step 2: BE BOLD:** Ask for what you need and then disengage from the outcome or how the solution will be provided. Be confident that the perfect outcome will arrive.
- **Step 3: BE STILL:** Allow God, or the universe, to act.
- **Step 4: BE AWARE:** Once you have asked for help, begin looking for and expecting the solution.

In the upcoming chapters, we will go through each step and I will explain each in more detail. The beauty of this program is in its simplicity. Those eight words cannot only change your outlook, but they can change your life.

Let's take a look at another small example:

Last year, my refrigerator started dying. I first noticed a problem when the ice cream began melting. This, of course, is practically a crime by itself! My refrigerator was 20 years old, so I figured that getting it repaired was not worth it. But something had to be done. I did not want to live out of a cooler in the garage. I was determined to get a new refrigerator before the current one completely stopped working.

I started out doing all of my usual research, spending lots of time and energy looking for the best model and price. I went to four or five stores and was having difficulty finding one that would fit in the space and had the features that I wanted. Of course, I also had a busy week at work and did not have a lot of time to go running all over town.

Just when things were getting really bad, I decided to let go of the struggle. A small shop that had been recommended to me almost 10 years before came to mind. Somehow, it had always stuck in my mind as a good place to buy appliances, even though I had never been there.

At this store, only two models would fit in the space in my kitchen. After looking at both of the refrigerators, there was really only one good option. So, without a lot of research or spending much energy, I decided to buy that refrigerator. It just felt right.

In the past, I would have been stressed because I wasn't finding what I wanted, and I would have used a lot more energy in looking for the best option. I would have been more anxious. But then I learned a new way of moving forward.

Here's how I approached the problem:

1. **Be Open:** I stopped worrying about needing to buy a new refrigerator. The cost and the inconvenience were not upsetting me. I accepted the situation and my feelings about it. I did not try to change anything about the present situation.
2. **Be Bold:** I asked God, or the universe, to have the best option provided to me. Then, I let go of any specific outcome.
3. **Be Still:** Since I had asked for help, I stopped thinking about what would happen. I stopped looking for the best brand, model, price, etc.
4. **Be Aware:** This last step was to wait for God (or the universe) to provide me with a solution.

This shopping experience had an unusual outcome. I became excited about getting a new refrigerator. I wasn't worried about the cost, even though it was a big purchase. When I went to pay for it and sign the paperwork, the clerk looked upset. She had just checked the availability a few minutes before; however, as she placed the order, the manufacturer indicated that this model was out of stock. It would not be available for at least six weeks. I was not worried. Why? Because I had asked for help and I knew that I would get the help I needed. So, I just stood there at the counter. I was *Being Still*. I didn't get worried or start calling my neighbors to see if I could borrow some space in their freezer.

The clerk checked again and had a puzzled look on her face. She said, "Wait, one just came available." She said, "I've never seen that happen before." She looked at me with surprise in her eyes. I just smiled and said, "It's magic."

She told me that it would be delivered in a few days. I was very happy about this and expected that everything would go according to plan. Two days later, just as I was leaving work early to meet the delivery van, I got a call from the store. The refrigerator had been delivered to them and was badly damaged and unusable.

I continued *Being Still* and waited to see what outcome was going to be presented to me. I was able to do this without getting upset because I was not attached to any particular outcome. Because the delay was not due to anything on my part, the store offered to bring me a loaner refrigerator for the next few weeks. They did this without any charge to me. I also got a discount on the refrigerator I had purchased because of my inconvenience. Within a few hours, I had a working refrigerator in my kitchen. Granted, it was kind of ugly and not at all what I would have chosen, but it was a loner after all. I ended up getting my new refrigerator delivered to me weeks later, at a reduced cost.

What happened? Why did the inventory show that there was not a refrigerator available and then it suddenly was in stock just a few minutes later? It's hard to say. What I know is that I had asked for help and I got it, including help with the cost. One key point is that I was open to however that assistance would be provided for me.

Think about a typical day for yourself. You get up in the morning, already feeling behind schedule. You rush to get yourself, and maybe the kids, ready for work and school. All the while, you're asking yourself these questions:

- *How am I going to get everything done today?*
- *What am I going to do about (this) or (that)?*
- *Why am I not getting any help, even though I asked for it?*
- *What am I doing all of this for?*

In addition to all those questions you have for yourself, you may also be organizing your day, going through your to-do list, and trying to determine what you can get done today and what can be put off for another day. You might have thoughts running through your mind: "I need to pick up one child from school and take them to soccer practice," and "How the heck am I going to get the other child across town to their ballet class?"

Or maybe you don't have young kids, and instead, you are focusing on the six tasks (or 12) that you have to get done at work. Maybe you're thinking about which one needs to be done first and which one your boss will be most unhappy with because it's not done. Or maybe you have young kids and deadlines at work and you're thinking about all of those things in the morning.

Then, add to all this inner dialogue the bigger questions and struggles you have in your life. Maybe you have a relationship that is not going well. Or you are constantly trying to figure out how you're going to pay your bills. Or you keep asking yourself how you are going to get all of this done and deal with your health problems at the same time. It's exhausting just thinking about it!

Now think about a different way of starting your morning.

- What if you did not worry about how you're going to get everything done?
- What if you were confident that things would work out financially?
- What if you knew that the best outcome for your relationship or your job difficulties would be provided to you?

What if you weren't worried because you knew that you were being given direction about each of these areas? And that you would end up with the perfect outcome, meeting all of your needs? That's where this formula **goes from being one that helps you in making decisions in your life to one that actually changes your life.**

If you could stop struggling so much in your life and stop spending so much energy worrying about how you are going to do what you need to get done, do you see your life changing? Close your eyes and imagine a day where you wake up in the morning and you get the kids ready for school and you get yourself ready for work, not worrying about the day ahead. You don't need to worry about how you're going to get everything done. You are not worried about how the boss is going to react. Doesn't that sound like a much better way to start your day?

Let's take a look at a common problem that many of you will probably identify with. Imagine that you are having difficulty with some aspect of your job. For example, your boss keeps giving you more and more responsibility, causing you to do more work, and you are not seeing any benefit to doing this. You are coming home later and later and you are getting more frustrated as each week goes by. You may want more pay for the extra work you are doing, or you might want to be doing less work. It doesn't matter.

What matters is that you are having difficulty at work and that you have some decisions to make. This example is put into four parts to show a close approximation of the four steps in the *Just Be* program.

Let's take a look at how many of us would normally try to solve a problem.

1. <u>The Problem:</u> Often, you can describe the problem at your job fairly easily. No doubt, you've told many friends and family about how much you don't like the situation. You may also be able to identify some of your feelings about the problem, especially your anger and frustration. But you are not accepting the situation. In fact, you want to do anything but accept the situation. You don't like it. It makes you angry. You are being taken advantage of by your boss.

Whatever is going on with you, it's likely that you're not accepting of the situation. Are you feeling grateful for your job at this point? Is it okay with you that you are working longer hours for the same pay?

It is also common to deny how you are really feeling about what is going on. You might be able to identify that you are angry. That's generally the easiest of emotions to identify. But could you admit to being sad? Scared? Grieving? Ashamed? If you can acknowledge some of those other feelings, are you judging yourself for having those feelings?

2. <u>What Outcome You Want:</u> If you started out by looking at where you are, then the next step is figuring out where you want to go. You may or may not have difficulty with this step. In this example, you might want fewer work responsibilities or more pay for the work you are doing. But let's add a few more questions to this.

- Do you want to stay in this job?
- Should you keep working there or start looking for a different job?
- Is there some other place that your soul is longing for?
- Should you just stay in this job until retirement and then pursue your dreams later?
- Should you set limits with your boss and tell him or her that you are not able to stay late on a regular basis?

Can you see how figuring out where you want to go may not be such a simple task? With an intimate relationship or partnership, it may be difficult to start considering whether or not you should end that relationship. This can all get very confusing and overwhelming, and in many cases, you could really struggle because you don't know what to do. You don't know what choice to make.

But, let's just say, for discussion's sake, that you know where you want to go. You want an increase in pay for the extra work that you are doing at your job, or you want to stay in the relationship that is not going so well right now. Okay, good. You know where you want to go. Do you know how to get there? Do you know if this is really the right decision?

Yes, you can continue trying and struggling and working under your own power. But I'm willing to bet that it doesn't always work out for you, and it takes a lot of energy. All of those mental gymnastics.

All the sleepless nights. All the stress of trying to figure out what to do. Aren't you tired of this?

3. <u>Try Harder:</u> Okay, so you've made your decision. You know the problem and you know what solution you want. What do you do now? This is the step where most people continue putting in more of their own energy. This is the step where people do the most work, and if things aren't getting resolved, then they work harder.

If you are spiritual, you are probably praying at this point. You might be talking to friends and confidants about what to do. You may even be taking some action. You could be making lists of the benefits and drawbacks of your situation. Maybe you are reading about how others have dealt with your particular problem.

In any case, you are probably engaging a lot of your own energy to try and get this problem solved. You are probably struggling, which is taking up time. This leads us to the last step.

4. <u>The Outcome:</u> What if your boss tells you that they are not going to give you an increase in pay for the extra work that you are doing? Then what? Do you just keep doing the extra work? Do you refuse to do it?

How about that relationship that is struggling? If you decide that you want to stay in it and fight for it, what about the other person? Are they going to fight for the relationship as much as you will? Do you really know which choice is the correct one?

Or maybe you are confident about which choice to make. You know what you want to do about your job or about your relationship, but you don't have full control of the outcome. You may want to continue a relationship, whether this is with a friend, a lover, or someone in your family. But you don't have ultimate control over the outcome of that relationship or about how strong that relationship will be in the future. You can set a limit with your boss and tell them that you are not going to do the extra work, but it's possible that your boss decides they don't want you to continue working there. Or you could ask for that raise, and your boss could say no. So, even if you are confident about the choice that you are going to make, the outcome is still out of your control. Then what?

The four steps that we just looked at in managing a problem in our lives is a typical example of the "old way" of addressing those issues. But now you will have an entirely different way, a new way.

4

The Struggle That is Common for Most of Us

Let's first take a look at the struggle that is common to most of us. Our focus is too often on wanting the things outside of us to change. We want a change in our job. We want a change in one or more of our relationships. We want a change in our income. This desire to have something in our external life change in order to feel better on the inside is a struggle that is common for most of us. However, changing our outside life does not generally result in a lasting change inside of us. It works the other way around. Instead, we actually need to heal ourselves from the inside out.

If you are not living your life in the direction
that your soul is pointing you toward, then you
will struggle.

Most of the clients that I have worked with are trying very hard to improve themselves and to live a life that lines up with their spirit or their soul. Where they are struggling is that they don't know how to line those two up. When you are struggling and not seeing progress, when your spirit is not aligned with the life you are living or when you are in a constant state of discontent...these are the things that drain your energy.

You are here because you keep trying and trying, struggling and struggling, and you need to find another way. Does any of this sound like you?

- *I'm trying to make my marriage work.*
- *I'm trying to make my boss happy.*
- *I'm trying to figure out whether I should quit my job and look for another one.*
- *I'm trying so hard to be a good parent.*
- *I'm trying to find a person to spend my life with.*
- *I'm trying to earn more money.*

Are you seeing the similarities in these sentences? Not only does the solution start with "I," but you are also putting in your own energy to make something change. You may be trying multiple ways of managing your problems. Then, if you find that one system doesn't work for you, you go on to the next one.

It is time to trade in,
"I'm trying to do this on my own," for,
"Someone else is handling it."

With all the effort that you are making in your life, do you feel like you are living the life you know you are meant to be living? How are you doing with the big three? Finances? Relationships? Health? One thing that I've discovered in my years of working with people who are having a rough time is that they are often struggling in more than one of these areas. A common belief that most people have is that they think life will only improve when they get what they desire. This is the struggle that is common for most of us.

Take a minute and think about what you keep hoping will change and what that change will bring you in your life.

You might say to yourself:
- *I'd be a lot happier if my child (friend, boss, coworker) stopped doing...*
- *I just need a different job.*
- *Once I move, it will get better.*

Or maybe it's about how you look:
- *If only I could lose weight, then I will...*
- *If only I were taller or prettier, then I would have...*

And then there's the big one:
- *If only I had more money!*

You have probably read that these changes won't really change your level of happiness or your level of contentment in your life. *And, secretly, you don't really believe that.*

You think, "If I won the lottery, and I had no more financial issues, I would find that peace and happiness that I'm looking for." And you may even joke to yourself that whatever problems came up, you'd be willing to tolerate them if you just had enough money. You think that you could buy your way out of most problems.

When I bring this up to my clients, and I mention that studies have shown that lottery winners are no happier than non-lottery winners, *I pretty much get a blank stare...and then an eye roll.*

You would be the exception, right? More money would make YOU happier. And, yes, there is an initial rise in the level of satisfaction immediately after winning a lottery, according to studies. But, within a few months that increase in the level of happiness goes back to previous, pre-lottery winning levels. In addition, many studies show that lottery winners file for bankruptcy at a higher rate than the average person. You may be saying right now, "Okay even if that's true, I'm willing to take that chance!"

Instead of trying to convince you that money doesn't buy happiness, I'd like to ask you to think about a time when you really wanted something and were sure that it would make you happy. Most of us have some example in our own lives, be it a relationship that we wanted, a new job, a new place to live, or a move to a different city.

Let's look at a particular job that you have considered. You might have been working at a low-paying job and you had your eye on another one that paid more money or maybe a promotion within the same company. The specific details aren't as important to this example as to how you felt about the outcome. Go ahead and change the specifics to fit your situation. Maybe you wanted to work for a competitor, or maybe you wanted to switch careers altogether. For this example, pick something that has already happened to you. We're looking at the outcome, so you need to find a situation where the outcome has already happened. Now think about that job that you did get, or that promotion, or that raise.

An example that comes to mind is a friend of mine who was waitressing for a popular restaurant in our hometown. She was very good at it and she liked what she was doing. But she was getting paid minimum wage and working for tips. She had higher aspirations. And, she worked nights. She spoke with me often about feeling discontented and wanting a different job. She wanted one that didn't rely on tips, had more income and better hours.

She applied for a manager's job in that same restaurant and got the position. She was a good waitress (I think she would correct me here and call herself a server), so I wasn't surprised that she was promoted. She was really happy that she'd gotten the promotion and she expected that her unhappiness would be wiped away by the increase in pay. Further, she believed that the elevated status would improve her sense of well-being. If she were asked to rate her level of overall happiness on a scale of 1 to 10, with 10 being ecstatic, I think she would have said she was around a 6. She liked her job as a server, so she wouldn't have said that she was completely unhappy. But the external things that she did not like about the job translated into her not being very happy with her life in general.

Can you guess what happened next? I'm not suggesting that promotions or new relationships or moves to new cities are bad. In fact, I'm not suggesting that at all. The point I'm making is that we have very high expectations for how happy an external situation will make us feel on the inside, once it changes. We generally believe that we will be so much happier and not struggle anymore once this situation or that person changes.

Well, my friend ended up being happy initially with her new promotion. She liked the things that she expected she would like. She worked daytime hours instead of every evening and on weekends. Her hourly rate increased. She now had staff! Her friends and her family congratulated her on becoming a manager at her young age. The promotion was not a bad thing. It was not a bad thing at all. However, it didn't actually change her sense of self, her level of happiness, or her overall contentment.

She hadn't focused on the fact that when you become a manager, you no longer get tips. And you no longer get paid for every hour you work. With her new promotion, because of the added responsibilities, her hourly rate actually dropped by a couple of dollars an hour. She had to come in early when there were problems on the job and she often stayed late. She soon realized that having staff wasn't all she thought it would be. The people that she now managed used to be her friends. She used to socialize with them. She used to make fun of the bosses with them. Now she was one of the bosses. Yes, she was working days instead of evenings. But if someone called in sick, she was expected to work in the evening as well. Even if she had worked all day.

I'm not giving this example as a way of saying, "Be careful what you ask for." I'm providing this example to show that we often have an image built up in our minds about how great things will be, and then the reality doesn't quite live up to those expectations. I would expect that my friend who had rated her happiness at about a 6 prior to the promotion, would still rate it about a 6 a few months later.

Looking back on it, she still would have pursued the promotion as there were benefits after all. The point of this example is, however, that we so often think one situation or one person is going to make all the difference in our lives. Life does not generally work that way.

Another example is when a person becomes a parent for the first time. Think back to when you had your first child. Being a parent is a fantastic role. As a new mother, you may have had thoughts about the joy of breastfeeding, the excitement of holding a new baby, or dressing up your young child. You think about the love you will have for your child. As a first-time father, you might have images of playing ball with your son or teaching him how to ride a bike. All of those images are wonderful, and those times that we spend with our children are precious.

Did you think about how much happier you would be once you had a child? Did you imagine that life would be much better? Now think about those first few months with your new child. The joy that you expected, the change in your life that you expected, the happiness that you knew this baby would bring you...Was that exactly what you thought it would be?

Maybe no one told you about how many dirty diapers your baby would produce, or what it would be like to go without sleep for the first four to six months. Where was the joy when your child was crying incessantly and everything you did to stop their tears failed to work? If you are a mother, did you expect the "baby blues?" How about the anxiety? Most people will tell you that having a child is a wonderful experience, one that brings you endless joy. And I agree.

Having a child may increase your level of happiness. However, I'm willing to bet it's not what you thought it would be. Maybe there was a lot more stress than you expected. Not because of your child. Not because parenting isn't a wonderful endeavor. But because it's hard.

I have talked with countless new moms who believed that every other new mom is just loving their baby and loving being a parent. They wonder why no one else is scared and anxious all the time, or they believe that they are the only mothers who are dealing with depression. They are wondering why they don't always love parenting as much as they thought they would. This is not because parenting is not a wonderful thing. **It's because we expect our external situation to vastly increase our level of happiness internally.** Your situation with having a child might be different and this example may not apply. That's okay. I've worked with enough new parents to know that it's going to resonate with many of you.

The bottom line is that we often think that a situation, a person, a job, a new residence, or a move to a new city is going to be the answer to all the problems we're dealing with now. And, in general, we find that many of the problems we had before those situations changed still exist. My point here is not to paint a depressing picture, but more to show how often we think that a change in our external environment will change how we feel internally. Some of those things do have an effect on us internally. I have worked with many people who felt that their happiness took a huge leap forward when they married the love of their life or when they had a child or when they found a job that they really enjoyed. Having more comfort in our life and feeling more secure absolutely can help us to feel happier.

On the flip side, there are many more times in our lives where we expect that an external change will bring about a lasting internal change and it just doesn't.

5

Trying to Change Someone Else

In the last chapter, we looked at wanting to change our external circumstances. In this chapter, we're going to take a deeper look at trying to change the people in our lives. Think about your spouse, your boyfriend or girlfriend, or any family member. If you are in any type of relationship, there are things about the other person that you want to change. No doubt. It's the human condition.

In fact, a huge part of my therapy practice starts with the request of my client wanting someone else in their life to change.

- *I want my husband to be...*
- *If only I had a wife who was...*
- *Can't my boyfriend just do this one thing?*
- *My mother is driving me nuts! She needs to stop doing...*
- *My boss is so...*

We think that we will be happier and more content if only the other person would change. There are two things wrong with this line of thinking.

The first error is to think that we have any power to change another person. Think about someone in your life whose behavior you would like to change. This could be a romantic partner, a friend, a sibling, or a parent. It shouldn't be too hard to find someone in your life who you want to act differently. Now think about all the times that you've tried to get them to act differently. How's that working for you?

I can give countless examples and I'm guessing that you can too. I have a client who has spent a lot of time telling me how she and her other family members would really prefer that another family member (her sister) would change her behavior and act differently. There have been many attempts to get her sister to change. A number of people in the family would like this sister to be more responsible. They would like her to be more "on top of things." They want her to return phone calls more quickly, pay her bills on time, stop dating "losers," and hold down a job. This woman is a bit of a hot mess. The effort to change her or wish that she were different generally has something to do with the wish for her to be more organized and more "together."

Of course, if you asked someone in that family why they want this woman to change, the first response is probably that they think that she would be happier if she wasn't always losing things, always late, not needing to pay late fees on her bills, not having her power turned off, etc. But the second reason why this family would want her to change is because of how it impacts their lives. And, let's be honest, this is really the first reason.

All behavior is functional.

One of the most common learnings that I share with my clients is that "all behavior is functional." This was first introduced to me by a professor in one of my psychology classes when I was an undergrad. At the end of this semester class, the professor, a psychologist, said, "If you remember one thing from this class, remember this. All behavior is functional." At first I thought that he was saying something very basic and I didn't get the importance of that sentence. But he went on to say, "Whenever you are working with a client or even talking to a friend or family member about their behavior, remember that all of us engage in our behaviors for a reason." It serves a function for us. If a behavior did nothing for us, we wouldn't do it. That concept has gotten me through more than one tough spot in my career.

There have been times when I have wondered how to help someone who is continuing to drink alcohol excessively or engage in another destructive behavior despite very clear evidence that it isn't working for them. I'm not talking about the physical addiction to alcohol. I'm talking about the person who has lost their house, their car, their job, and their family. They have lost everything and they're still not interested in addressing the cause of those losses, their physical addiction to alcohol. This is the step before treating the physical addiction.

The concept that all behavior serves a purpose is a description of all behavior, not just the significantly self-destructive behavior. If you are constantly late for appointments, there is some function in that behavior that serves a purpose for you. If you are a meticulous housekeeper, there's a purpose in there as well.

Getting back to my client's family member... Since all behavior serves a purpose, it would be helpful to look at this situation within the same framework. On some level, this woman's behavior is serving a purpose for her. I'm not going to begin to try and figure out what that is. However, I don't think that she's really unhappy with who she is. It's more that the people around her are unhappy with her behavior. And isn't this how it often is? When we want someone near to us to behave differently or act differently, we are generally doing that because of how their behavior impacts us. Their behavior probably does not bother them significantly. Or else they would change it. So, isn't this really our problem and not theirs?

Can you guess the outcome of this situation? In all the years I've known about the sister, she has acted fairly consistently. All the requests and demands to have her act differently have just resulted in frustration and bad feelings in her family. Not one of them has resulted in the sister changing her behavior. Why is that? Because we have no authority, whatsoever, to change another person. People can change, of course. But people will change because they choose to change themselves. We cannot change other people. This is a big one! It's really hard not to want to change those around us. But trying to change others is a losing battle.

There are going to be some of you who will think of a situation where others were successful in getting the behavior of someone else to change. I agree that this may appear to be true in some cases. When we are successful in getting another person to change their behavior, it is almost always because there is a difference in the balance of power between the two parties. For example, between a boss and an employee. When there is such a difference in power in a relationship, the person who wields the power can, in fact, force change. However, this is still a losing battle. Why? This is because we may be able to force a change in behavior by overpowering someone, but the outcome has interpersonal consequences.

In this example, a boss may be able to require that a consistently tardy employee arrives to work on time. The boss may be able to force this change because the employee does not want to lose their job or have their pay docked. In a business situation, this forced change can work. The employee may change their behavior and begin arriving to work on time. However, the boss will not have had any effect on the employee's attitude. In fact, the employee may become resentful or irritable. You may even find that the employee becomes passive aggressive in their behavior. Why is that? Because the change in behavior was forced due to that power differential. The employee probably did not want to change their behavior, or else they would have done it earlier. They feel forced to do something they did not want to do. So they do it, but feeling that they had no choice, they can become resentful or angry.

This four-step system *(1. Be Open 2. Be Bold 3. Be Still 4. Be Aware)* will show you a new way of addressing your own life challenges. The focus is never on changing someone else so that you can have an easier go of things. It doesn't work out that way.

Let's get back to the idea of wanting someone else to change their behavior in order for you to be happier. The first problem with this line of thinking is that you cannot change the behavior of another person. Not without their consent. The second problem is that it will not increase your level of happiness.

In working with spouses, the most common phrase I hear from each of them is, "I want them to do this differently," or "I want them to stop doing that." And yes, if their spouse made those changes, there would be an initial relief and some stress reduction. However, in a very short period of time, you would just find the next thing you want to change in that person. You might even move on to another person who you believe needs changing.

If a person does choose to make a change in their behavior, you will find that the change may initially make you feel happier. By having open and honest discussions with loved ones about how we are feeling, the other person may choose to make a behavior change because they care about you. You can then experience less stress and feel like they are listening to your needs and caring for you. These are all good things. These are all things that we would want to see in a relationship. However, you will find that after a while, it doesn't solve all the problems that you thought it would.

Your sense of happiness may be fleeting. Why is that? Well, first, because there is an endless supply of things that we would like to change in other people. Second, the problem does not really lie in someone else's behavior. We are bothered by the behavior of someone else because of something we don't like or do not accept in ourselves.

Let's look at this idea. If your partner is always flirtatious and this makes you jealous, you may say that you want them to stop being so flirtatious with other people. You want their behavior to change. If we are considering the premise that what we don't like in other people is really what we don't like in ourselves, let's look at what we might not like in ourselves when our partner is being flirtatious. We may feel that we are not good enough, pretty enough, or smart enough. This gets highlighted when we see our partner flirt with someone else. Even if we could get our partner to stop being flirtatious all together, that would not eliminate our own feelings of inadequacy. Do you see how that works?

Just because our partner's behavior changed, we still have the issue that we are struggling with inside of ourselves. What you end up with is a partner who is trying to please you by not doing something and then you are not really feeling any happier because of it. This can result in a lot of frustration between the two of you. The partner probably doesn't think they were doing anything wrong. And you think that their behavior change will bring about happiness and contentment to yourself, but then it doesn't. This can leave you confused, maybe even angry.

Are you starting to see why this doesn't work? If the real problem is how you feel about yourself, then having your partner change one aspect of their behavior isn't going to change very much. Yes, you may feel a little bit better when you go out with your partner and they are not flirting with other people. However, it isn't going to make a big difference since the issue you are really dealing with is your own self-worth.

Your partner may also feel resentful that you have asked them to change their behavior. Think about it. If you said to your partner, "I don't like how flirtatious you are when we are out," or "I don't like how much you flirt with other people." How do you think they would react? Do you think that your partner would agree with you and say, "Yes, you're right, I flirt with other people and that is not nice." Or are they more likely to say, "I don't do that," or, "I do that because you don't pay attention to me?" Or maybe they'd even say, "It's just harmless fun."

Trying to change someone else not only rarely works, but it almost never brings us the outcome that we are looking for. And, yet we keep trying. Am I right?

Why do we keep trying to change other people? Well, that's a loaded question. However, the short answer is because we keep having the same problems within ourselves that aren't going away, so we keep trying to make ourselves feel better.

We keep hoping that something in our external life will change. We keep hoping for that change because something in our internal life is not going well. We are not content. We are not happy. We are not at peace. How many books have you read on this subject? How many people have you talked to about finding peace and contentment in your life? How many things have you tried? I'm guessing that you are reading this book today because, at some level, the things you've tried in the past haven't worked very well. Let's consider a radical concept...

Accept your current situation and stop trying so hard to change the outside.

6

Accepting Where You Are

Let's try something completely different from what you've tried before. Try accepting where you are. Accept how you are feeling. Accept those parts of you that you are not particularly pleased with. Then, work towards understanding that you are right where you are supposed to be.

Accepting how you're feeling starts with knowing what you're feeling. I find that many of my clients have a very difficult time identifying what they are feeling. Generally, most of us can identify anger. It's an acceptable feeling in our society. But when was the last time you admitted to feeling sad or scared? And how often do we like to admit that we feel guilty, inadequate, ashamed or humiliated?

Happy feelings are not too difficult to be aware of and acknowledge. The negative ones? Oh, those are more difficult. We don't like to admit how unhappy we are feeling. And because we don't spend a lot of time there, we have a difficult time even being able to identify our negative feelings. Acknowledging how you are feeling is step one. Then, accepting that those feelings are okay and not judging yourself for them is step two.

When we are in some type of pain, whether that is physical pain or emotional pain, the first thing that we want to do is get rid of it. And why not? It's painful! But, if you keep trying to do the same thing over and over again, guess where that gets you? Why not try something different? Why not try accepting your situation?

First, what you've been doing isn't working. That lends itself to trying something different. Second, I am in no way suggesting that your goal should be to continue to stay in the pain or the discomfort or the negative situation. Nor am I suggesting that you should continue to feel bad about yourself. What I am suggesting is that you accept the reality of the situation that you are in right at this moment.

Stop fighting your current reality.

Take, for example, that your relationship with your significant other is really not going well. You two may have been trying to make it work for a while. You may find yourself ignoring those telltale signs that keep creeping up, letting you know that things are not good.

Do you find that it's easier to see someone else's problem or the solution to their problem than it is to see your own? We can often see a friend's relationship going downhill long before we see our own. Why is that? Because we have blind spots. We don't like to swim in the pool of discomfort, so we pretend we're not swimming there at all. I'm willing to bet that you can think of more than one situation where you should have stepped away long before you did, or after you quit a stressful job, you said to yourself, "I should have left years ago."

Let's consider a very simple example of getting a flat tire. You are driving along, minding your own business, and you notice that the car starts pulling a little to the right. If you have your windows open, you might hear the sound of the tires on the road change a little. If your first thought is, "No, nothing is wrong. I'm just going to keep driving," does this change whether the tire is going flat or not? What happens if you keep driving and the car continues to get harder to steer? Your car might start flashing a warning sign on the dashboard that you have low tire pressure. Still, you continue to say to yourself, "I don't want to deal with this situation. I don't like having a flat tire, so I'm just going to ignore it."

If we continue with this example, you might reach a place where the car is next to impossible to steer with a completely flat tire. Maybe you pull off the road because of this. But if you are continuing to deny that you have a flat tire, it isn't changing whether that is true or not. You could say to yourself all you want, "I don't have a flat tire because I don't want to have a flat tire," or, "I'm just going to close my eyes and wish it away." Does that change how much air pressure is in your tire? Does it change the reality of your situation?

If you look at a relationship like a car tire, you might find that your relationship is losing air and going flat. Your friends around you can see that the tire (your relationship) is deflating, but you may continue to deny that this is true. You can want and wish that the tire is not going flat, but that does nothing to change the situation. When you accept a situation as it is, it does not mean that you want the situation to stay that way. It does not mean that you do not want a different outcome. However, if your relationship "tire" is going flat, denying that it is does not change the reality of the situation.

If you notice the low air pressure in the tire or the warning light on your dashboard and say to yourself, "Oh, I have a flat tire," you can pull over to the side of the road and deal with the reality of the situation. Believing you have a flat tire or denying that you have a flat tire does not change whether or not the tire is flat. The situations that we experience in our lives are just that. They are the situations that they are. Your choice is how you address that situation. **Denying that a situation exists does not change that it exists.**

Another way of looking at this is to think about the concept of holding a hot coal in the palm of your hand. If you were to take a hot coal out of your barbecue and put it in your outstretched palm, it would hurt. Think of that hot coal as a negative situation in your life. It hurts; it's painful. But what if you clench your fist and squeeze that hot coal tightly within your hand? It would end up hurting more. You would end up burning more of your hand. By grasping and struggling and fighting against that negative situation, we end up burning ourselves even more. But if we allow that hot coal to just sit there on the palm of our hand, a few things can happen.

First, it is touching the least amount of skin that it can and therefore burning us less than if we made a fist around the coal. Second, if we allow the coal to be there in the open air and not add any more fuel, the fire will burn out.

I am sure that there is at least one of you who is saying, "The coal hurts. Why would I allow it to stay in my hand? Why don't I just throw it on the ground?" And, in actuality, that's what most of us do. We have something in our life, some feeling, some situation, and we don't like how it feels, so we just toss the feeling away. But if we are going to stick with this analogy, I'd suggest that you look down on the ground.

The hot coal hasn't really gone away.
It's still there.
And you will step on it eventually.

7

Step 1: Be Open

Let's take a deeper look at the first of the four steps – *Be Open*. This step is about being open to your current situation. Anytime we have a negative situation in our life or a negative feeling, it's very common that the first thing we do is to jump right into getting rid of that feeling or that situation. And why not? It is painful or uncomfortable. However, jumping over this first step throws the whole process off.

How often have you been going through your day and you start to get just a little bit of a scratchy throat? Maybe you feel slightly run down? Maybe you even feel a little bit warmer than usual. Are you someone who says, "No, I am not getting sick. I don't have time to get sick. I can't afford to get sick," and then you just keep going? The next day you wake up and maybe you have a few more symptoms, but you go about your same routine because, after all, you are not really sick.

Let's consider another example. Maybe your living situation is not acceptable. It might be the wrong neighborhood, a bad neighbor who isn't going to move, or you might be living in a house you cannot afford. Do you spend a lot of time telling yourself, "It isn't that bad?" Do you tell yourself, "I'm not really that unhappy," or, "At least I don't have to deal with...?" Or maybe you tell yourself, "This is really as good as it's going to get," even if it's not very good.

In these two examples, do you see where the person is just pushing away how they are feeling? Or that they are denying the current situation? How many times have you spoken to a friend about a situation that they aren't willing to face and you have told them that the problem is right in front of their eyes? Why is it so much easier for us to see a friend's problem than it is for them to see the problem for themselves?

I call this the Ostrich Approach. So often we think that if we bury our head in the sand, the problem will just go away. But it doesn't, does it? Just like the flat tire that we want to deny having—refusing to admit that a situation exists does not change the situation.

Let's get back to Step 1. *Being Open* is accepting and agreeing with your current situation. It does not have to be your preference, but you do need to be aware of your circumstances.

You can't fix what you don't acknowledge.

You can't deal with a situation that you don't even admit exists. The first part is to admit what is going on. The next part is to be honest about how you are feeling about it.

If we are looking at the example of a marriage that is in trouble, you would first have to face that you are not happy in the relationship or that there are problems in the relationship. Nothing can be changed until you acknowledge the situation that you are in.

To put it another way…you can't get where you want to go if you don't know where you are starting from. Even the travel websites know this.

If you want to fly to New York, the first thing you need to do is to type in your starting point. You cannot book the flight to New York without first entering the airport you are starting from.

If your destination in your marriage is to feel happier, more secure, or more content, then you need to know where you're starting from. And the only way to know where you're starting from is to be honest with where you are standing right now. This can be tough. Those two little words, *"Be Open,"* have a lot of power to them.

> Be Open: Accept and agree with the situation; including your feelings about the situation.

Accepting the situation is not just acknowledging that it exists, but being okay that you are going through it.

When we have a hot coal burning our hand, we want to throw it down on the ground. We don't want to stand there and look at it, and we certainly don't want to accept that we have a painful situation in our hand. But, *Being Open* is exactly this. It's the acknowledgment that the situation you are in is exactly where you are supposed to be right now. It's not comfortable. It doesn't feel good. But it's where you are supposed to be. Is it where you were supposed to end up? Probably not. **Being Open is accepting your current state of affairs.** It is not only acknowledging that your marriage is in trouble but being okay with it.

This is not where most of us start out, right? We want to push away the uncomfortable feelings. We want to deny the negative situation. We do not want to be okay with it. And, this is exactly where you need to start.

One of the most common misunderstandings I run into with this step is that my client thinks it means that they want the bad situation to continue. I often get pushback at this point.

- *But I don't want to be in a failing marriage.*
- *I don't want to have this illness.*
- *I certainly don't want to have financial problems.*

Accepting that a situation exists and wanting that situation to exist are two different things. Let's take the example of being late for an important meeting. If you are driving to a meeting, looking at the clock, and realizing that you are not going to get there on time, you could be pretty upset. You don't want this situation to exist. Can you agree that it does exist? You are going to be late for the meeting. That's the reality. It doesn't mean you want it. It just means that you are acknowledging the reality of the situation. You are not denying that it is true. You have accepted that you are going to be late for an important meeting. You may feel angry about this. You may be anxious. You could even get defensive, coming up with all sorts of reasons that you're going to tell your boss why you showed up late.

Or, you could try a different approach.

You could stop fighting it and just accept that you are going to be late for the meeting. You can drop the anxiety, the anger, and the defensiveness. You can both surrender to the situation and take responsibility for it.

This starts by saying to yourself, "Yes, I'm going to be late for this meeting." Then, acknowledging how you feel about that. You may still be anxious and angry about it. The difference is accepting that you are feeling anxious and angry about it. You are not trying to change the situation. Accept that you are on the road and you are heading to an important meeting and you will be late for that meeting. And that's okay.

In addition, refrain from blaming things outside of yourself for your situation. If you spend your time driving to work blaming others and being angry with your kids, your spouse, the traffic, etc., then you are still not accepting your current situation. Focusing on how much you feel victimized by those circumstances keeps you from *Being Open*.

8

Step 2: Be Bold

Let's go back to our exercise about finding a flight to New York. If Step 1: Be Open, is about looking at where you're starting from, then, Step 2 is your New York. It's where you want to go.

Being Bold involves making a statement about what you want and where you want to go. But this can be misinterpreted, so let's break it down a little. It's not about being demanding. Nor is it about insisting. The "bold" in Step 2 is about confidence and faith. It's stating your desire and then having the confidence that you will get the response that you need. It's not a wish, because wishes can go either way. You can either get your wish or not get your wish. However, when you are connecting with the greatest power in the universe, you can be confident that you will get the help you need.

It's easy to start thinking about what you want in terms of things. This could be a change in your job, more money, a new relationship, or it could be in more tangible objects like a new TV or a new car. However, in order to take this program from a small decision-making technique to one that changes your life, think in terms of how you want to feel.

Imagine the life that you really want to be living. Yes, you can look at what you own or where you live in that life. But, I challenge you to also look at how you are feeling. Do you feel content? Are you calm? Do you feel a sense of security? How would you act in this new life? Are you a giving person? What type of a friend or lover are you?

When you are boldly stating what you want, don't just think about what you want in terms of physical things; think about where you want to go. What is your "New York?"

Think back to when you were a small child, about three or four years old, and you asked an adult to help you tie your shoe. Was that a wish? Did you expect them to say no? Yes, you were making a request, but you really expected them to help you.

Consider another example of a time when you were carrying something heavy and you were walking near someone you knew. Then, both of you arrived at a door around the same time. You asked them to open the door for you. It's obvious that you would have had a difficult time opening the door for yourself because your hands were full. Did you expect them to say no? Or was your expectation that they would help you?

In these two examples, help with getting your shoes tied or help with opening a door when your hands are full, your expectation is that you will get the help that you need. You would ask with confidence. You are expecting that the answer to be "yes."

Let's take a look at the other side of this situation. Think about a time when you have asked someone for assistance when you weren't very confident that they would help you. This might have been a person with whom you had a complicated relationship. It might have been with a person whom you did not know very well, or you were making a request that could have been more than they had to offer at the time.

For example, consider asking a friend to loan you a few hundred dollars. If you are making a request where you think the answer could go either way, do you find yourself asking more hesitantly? Or less confidently? And, if you are making a request of someone where you expect them to offer the help you are asking for, are you more confident? More bold in your request? Not demanding, but confident that they will help you. That's why Step 2 is about *Being Bold.* It's stating your desires, or your request, with confidence. It's confidently expecting that you will get the assistance you've asked for.

There's a second part to this step that is **more important than the first part.** You need to let go of how that help will come to you. Think about needing a new car because yours is old and keeps breaking down. But, you demand that you want a bright red, shiny, top-of-the-line sports car with all the bells and whistles, and the only outcome that is acceptable to you is that one car, with that one color, given to you in the next two weeks. In this scenario, I'm fairly confident in telling you that you may not get it.

However, if you boldly state to God or the universe that you need a new car because you need help in getting to work and getting around town, then you let go of how that car will get delivered to you, when you will get it, and what type of car it will be. Your chances of getting the perfect outcome just increased significantly. It's easy to worry and be anxious at this point that you might get a car, but it will be broken down and ugly. That is just fear talking. The universe does not desire to work against you.

Think back to the three-year-old who asks for help with having their shoe tied. Maybe the child was on the playground and you, as their parent, decided that they really didn't need to wear shoes right at that time. So you lean down and say, "Hey, let's take off your shoes and run around barefoot." Or, maybe that same child just walked outside in the rain and you saw puddles all around. Instead of tying their shoe right at that moment and getting both of you wet, you pick them up and carry them inside to a safer and drier place.

In both of those scenarios, that three-year old's shoe did not get tied. At least not right away. Do you think that was a problem for the child? Probably not. Why? Because their request was based on a need not to trip over their shoelace or not to have their shoe fall off. If you met that need by telling them that they did not need to wear shoes at that time or by picking them up and moving them to a drier location, then whether or not the shoe gets tied right at that moment becomes less important.

The request was to have their shoe tied, but the solution was better. They got to run around in the grass barefoot. They got scooped up quickly and taken out of the rain instead of merely having someone tie their shoe. If the child is open to a variety of outcomes, the outcome may not look like they had originally thought, it could be even better! The solution not only met the physical request—their untied shoe—but also the emotional needs of being cared for and experiencing joy. The child got their needs met. Just not in the way that they originally requested.

The outcome may not look like you think it will.
It could be even better!

Now if you've been around children for any length of time, you've probably met that child who is not open to a variety of outcomes. Think about the child who asks you to tie their shoe and then does not want any other outcome than to have you bend down and tie their shoe immediately. Even if it means that both of you are standing in the rain. If that child holds tightly to their solution being the only solution and will not allow any other outcome, then you are going to end up with an unhappy child. The difference here is that of a child holding tightly to only one acceptable outcome versus a child who has a need and is open to a variety of ways that their need can be met. They made a request, with confidence, of what they needed and then let go of how that solution had to come.

Can you think of a time in your life when you wanted something badly? A relationship with a particular person? A certain job? That new handbag? Then, think of a time when you got exactly what it was that you wanted. Those times can be fantastic.

Can you also think of a time when you got exactly what you wanted, and it wasn't really what you needed? Or the flip side of that, when you did not get something that you really wanted and that was exactly what you needed!

Most people I know can come up with some very clear examples in their own life. Have you said or ever heard a friend say something like one of these statements:

- *Losing that job was the best thing that ever happened to me.*
- *When I got evicted from my apartment, I was devastated, but it turned out to be the best move for me.*
- *Wow, I dodged a bullet when that person broke up with me. Even though it hurt at the time.*

Sometimes, things that seem negative at the beginning don't end up being negative. We often think we know exactly what we want. But there are times that getting it really isn't the solution that we needed. In boldly stating what you want and then allowing God, or the universe, to give you what you really need, you are letting the outcome be determined by a power much greater than yourself. Who do you want to provide the solution? You, your ego, and your own limited brain? Or the power that runs the entire universe?

In boldly stating what it is that you want, be careful that you don't put God, or the universe, into the role of being your very own personal Santa Claus. Stating your desires is about getting clear on what it is you truly want. It's not about creating a shopping list that the universe or God needs to fulfill in a specific amount of time. It's easy to do this because this is where our ego wants to go. In connecting to a power greater than ourselves, we need to also acknowledge that this power knows more than we do. Just like the three-year-old who sees their shoe untied, the adult knows the greater need of getting out of the rain.

To sum up, ***Being Bold* is confidently stating what you need, having faith that your needs will be met, and then letting go of how that solution will be provided.**

Although this step involves determining your need, the more important component is not being invested in the outcome. The "boldness" of this step is having confidence that you will be provided for. And, yes, this does require faith. Faith that God, or the universe, is listening to you and knows what you need.

9

Faith

Let's take a look at faith and spirituality. Faith makes many people think of religion. In fact, all religions talk about faith. Faith is believing in a power greater than ourselves. Faith can also be applied to situations where you have no control.

When you get on an airplane, you have faith that the pilot knows what they are doing and will fly you to your destination. You also have faith that the plane is in good working condition so that it will fly safely. If you really have strong faith, you also believe that your luggage will arrive at the same destination that you do!

If you did not have faith that the pilot was skilled or that the plane was safe to be flown, you would not get on that plane. Think about it. If you saw the pilot sitting at a bar clearly inebriated before your flight, then you would not get on that plane, would you? Because you did not have faith that they were competent to fly the plane.

The Strength and Power of the Universe

The universe has tremendous power. Consider the waves in the ocean, earthquakes, hurricanes, or the temperature of the sun. The gravitational pull of the Moon and the Sun make the water in the oceans rise and recede, creating waves. Have you ever considered the awesome power of a large storm? Or that water and wind created the Grand Canyon by moving through rocks?

Stand at the edge of the ocean and look out at the sea. Then compare yourself to this power. Is there anything in your body or in your own will, that has the enormous power of the ocean? Have you ever felt that small? Mother Earth is one powerful lady!

How about our solar system? Take a look at an image of our solar system and consider how small the Earth is compared to the other planets around it. Saturn is nearly 1,000 times the size of the Earth. And the sun is so large in comparison to our planet that 1.3 million Earths could fit inside the Sun.

Why not harness that power? Think of your own power, coming just from you, the things you have control of and can impact. Compare that to the power of the universe. Whether or not you believe that God is the creator of this universe, most of us can acknowledge that there is a power far greater than ourselves at work.

This program involves having faith in something greater than yourself. This may be God. You may consider it to be universal energy or a higher power. It can be whatever connects with you. The focus is on the origin of the energy and what power you connect with.

Are you trying to do all of this by yourself? Are you trying hard to get your life in order? Can you let go long enough for God or the universe to provide? Connecting to this power, allowing it to step in and lead the way, can have a tremendous impact on your life.

If you begin struggling in your life, look at your faith in that power. Regardless of where you think the power of the universe comes from or what you call it, when you start questioning that power, you will begin struggling.

When you are stating your need, you boldly state your need with confidence because you have full faith that your need will be met. Your doubt in the power or your fear that you won't get what you need can absolutely impact how well these steps work.

Think about a surfer out in the ocean ready to catch that next wave. That wave is powerful, right? The wave has the power to carry a person on a surfboard to shore. In fact, when surfing, it's the wave that does most of the work.

What happens if that surfer begins to doubt in the power of that wave? What happens if he is hesitant in getting on his board or how to position himself so that he can catch the wave for its full impact? If he doesn't trust that the wave is coming or that the wave has the power to support him, he's going to have a pretty difficult time surfing. It's not that the ocean lacks power. It is not about the skill of the surfer. However, if the surfer begins to doubt that the ocean can help carry him, then he will be unable to get where he wants to go.

Fighting the power of the universe is like trying to stop a wave, or alter an earthquake, or stop the path of a tornado.

Quit trying to be in charge of the universe.

If you are trying to manage your life on your own or figure it out for yourself, you are doing it without the power of the universe.

Think back to the last time you stood at the edge of the ocean and watched the waves roll in. Can you imagine trying to make that happen on your own or telling the ocean that you know a better way to get the water to shore? Would you try telling the ocean that you are going to take care of things on your own and that you don't need the power of the universe to help you?

10

Step 3: Be Still

We are at the third step which is about *Being Still*. This is probably the most important step. And it may be the hardest step. Why? Because it's about letting go of control. It's having faith that the power we just spoke about in the last chapter is going to provide for you. And the key here is to truly let go of trying to solve the problem. I know from personal experience that this is much easier said than done. My own struggle with this step is not that I have such a hard time asking God for assistance or help with my problem. I can generally do that okay. My struggle is that I keep taking the problem back again because God isn't working fast enough!

You may have difficulty letting go in the first place. Maybe you have difficulty in trusting that God or the universe is going to provide for you. Wherever the difficulty, this step can be tough. **Being Still is letting go of the illusion of control.** This step takes practice. However, the results are tremendous.

I get a lot of feedback about this step. People ask, "So, I'm just supposed to do nothing? I just sit on the couch and all of my problems will be solved?" Absolutely not!

The first part of *Being Still* is to stop trying to figure out for yourself how you—and you alone—are going to solve this problem. This is the step where you engage in the power available to you through the universe. Continuing to try and figure out what you are going to do keeps the problem in your hands. *Being Still* is letting go of that illusion of control.

This step could be confusing to you if you were wondering why, in Step 2, you stated where you wanted to go. And now it looks like you are removing that step. This is a good point to understand. Boldly stating what you want and where you want to go is about having confidence that God or the universe will get you there. It is not about insisting on where you are going.

In Step 3: Being Still, your role is to surrender your ego's desire for control and allow something larger than yourself to take over. It's not about giving up. **This is actually a power move.**

In this step, you may be very busy. You may have a lot to do. But your "doing" is not about solving the problem that was outlined in the first two steps.

The second part of *Being Still* is to begin acting as if you have received the outcome you were looking for. If you have asked the universe or God for assistance in getting you a new job, then you would begin acting as if that new job were right around the corner. You need to start preparing for the change. That's the action part in *Being Still.*

If you want a relationship to improve, begin acting how you would act if that relationship were already better.

This is important because you don't want to come from a place of doubt. You want to come from a place of confidence that the power you just connected with is doing exactly what you need.

Think back to that small example where you are carrying a heavy package and you have asked a friend if they would open a door for you. Since you are confident that this friend will help you, you would act as if the help were coming. You would not set down the heavy package, expecting to have to open the door yourself. You would not look around and ask three more people to open the door for you. If you have confidence that your request will be fulfilled, then you will act as if it is fulfilled. In fact, that package might begin to feel a little lighter because you know you aren't going to have to juggle the heavy load and try to open the door by yourself. And when you get to the door, your expectation is that it will be opened for you.

You are coming from a place where your
problem has already been solved.

If you ask a family member to pick up dinner on the
way home from work and you are confident that
they will do that for you, then you don't have to
spend the rest of the day worrying about what
you're going to do about dinner. You would act as if
that need were already met, even though you are
hours away from dinner. If you don't trust the
person that you asked to follow through, then you
would continue worrying or thinking about what
you are going to do about dinner. If you have faith
that what you asked for will be delivered, then you
can let it go and focus on other things. That's what
Being Still is all about. Once you have asked for the
help, you can have the confidence that you will get
what you need. You don't have to spend all of your
time worrying about how that will happen.

11

When You Find Yourself Struggling

When you find yourself struggling, the goal is not to add more to your situation. It's easy to start thinking about "doing" one more thing or trying harder to get what you want. The focus should be on removing what you don't need.

Think about the image of carrying around a backpack full of rocks. These are the difficulties that we carry around with us. Our baggage. Our "issues." Many of us have a lot of rocks in those backpacks. And we are carrying them around with us wherever we go.

The first thing to do is to realize what rocks you carry with you. You can't change what you don't know. This is always a good place to start. When you know what you are dealing with, the goal is to lighten your load. It's time to remove some of the rocks in your backpack.

So much of the time, what we do instead is take a rock out of our backpack, look at it, and roll it around in our hands a little bit. We feel the ridges, or the smoothness, or the imperfections of that rock. We get a sense of how heavy it is. We try to learn more about our rock. And we may learn, "I have issues with jealousy," or "I feel insecure," or "I have low self-esteem."

It's what we do next that helps to lighten our load or not. If we take that learning, and we put the rock back in our backpack, secure in the knowledge that we have learned something, then we haven't lightened our load one single bit!

This is where books, self-help courses, and even some well-meaning coaches, friends, or family fall short when trying to help. Sure, we want direction on what decision to make. We want help to know whether to stay in our dead-end job because it's safe and secure or to branch out and try a different career. We want direction on how our marriage can be better. Or we want to know if we would really be happier leaving our spouse or leaving a relationship.

If you don't make the changes, then nothing really changes.

Let's look at an example. Think about having a job that you're not happy with and your question is whether you should leave that job and look for another one. The reason you stay is that it's comfortable. The pay is adequate for what you do. You like most of your coworkers. The reasons to leave are that you could be making more money or you could find more satisfying work.

The barriers to leaving? These are the big ones, right? Do you leave what's comfortable, what is safe? Do you step into a job where you don't know your coworkers and you don't know what the new boss would be like? Do you do this in hopes of finding a better job? Who of us has not been in a similar situation?

This is where humans have their limitations. When you are looking for direction, you probably did not just go to one person, did you? You probably asked the advice of many friends. You may have even read several books or looked online for hours. In the end, you may have chosen to stay or to leave your job, but you weren't absolutely sure that the decision you made was the right one.

Now you can turn to someone or something and have confidence that the direction you are given is the best direction. Isn't that the better way to go? You can still talk with family and friends. However, connecting with the power of the universe is connecting with the ultimate authority pointing you in the right direction. You can feel confident that the assistance you are given is always the right assistance. This is how to take some of those rocks out of your backpack and lighten your load. This is why *Being Still* is such an important step. You take some rocks out of your backpack and hand them over to God or to the universe. You let go of the need to solve it yourself.

Being Still is stopping the effort of trying to solve problems on your own.

What to Do if You Get Stuck

In *Being Still* you let go of fear, embrace the calm, and have faith that your higher power is handling the situation. But what do you do when you find yourself struggling? I'm sure you already know that just telling yourself to calm down or let go of what you were holding onto doesn't work so well. When you look back on the concept that "all behavior is functional," you can begin to understand why it's not so easy to just stop struggling. The struggling has a function, and there's a good possibility that the reason you are struggling is fear. When you get to a point where you say, "This process isn't working," or, "I can't do the steps. I can't just *Be Still.*" This is where you need to look at what is keeping you from moving forward.

There are a number of different places where you can get yourself off track in this program. In Step 3: Be Still, you may encounter some of those obstacles. You might start out by letting go of your problem and asking God to take over. But then you take the problem back because you find it isn't being solved in the way you want it done, or you just might find yourself getting discouraged and losing faith.

Letting go of trying to find the solution to your problem requires that you let go fully. Ask yourself,

"Am I okay with any outcome that the universe provides?" Or, "I have asked for help with my relationship, but am I okay with that relationship continuing or ending? Do I trust that God or the universe is going to provide in the best way possible?"

When you find yourself grasping for a particular outcome or unable to let go of attachment, the first thing to do is look at what you are afraid of.

- If you can't see what you are afraid of, look at what you are worried about losing.
- If you still can't see what you are afraid of, imagine not getting the outcome that you want.
- Then, ask yourself how that feels. From there you can look at what you are afraid of.

Let's look at some examples to get a better idea. Imagine yourself in a relationship, and you really want that relationship to work. In fact, you're working very hard on making it work. If you truly were honest with yourself, you would be able to see that you are struggling in that relationship. You and your partner are just not on the same page, but you are hanging on tight. You want the white picket fence, the 2.5 kids, and the minivan. You want it all. And he's a good person and a good provider, or you want someone who you know will be a good mother to your children. So you hang in there. You keep trying. In fact, you try harder.

Here is where I would ask you what you are afraid of. You might say that you are afraid of the relationship ending. But let's push that one a little bit more and ask what scares you about the relationship ending. After some thought, you answer that you are afraid you are not going to get what you really want...the picket fence and the smiling children. If this is the case, imagine yourself without the picket fence and the children. Imagine yourself alone, unmarried, and not living in the suburbs.

If imagining yourself without those outcomes makes you uncomfortable, then you will start to be able to see where your fear is. Once you acknowledge your fear, you should be able to see what is holding you back from fully letting go of the outcome and handing it over to your higher power.

Another example might have to do with your job. You have a good paying job. A job that you are good at. You have good relationships at work and your coworkers respect you. You live in a nice house and your family is taken care of. But the job is nipping at your heels. In fact, you're coming home angry every night. You are frustrated that this good, stable, well-paying job is something you might consider leaving. But you have responsibilities. You have bills. Now you find yourself stuck. You don't know what to do.

You start by *Being Open* (Step 1). You can finally acknowledge that you have been telling yourself you are supposed to like your job and you now admit that you really don't. You acknowledge that the money you are making at the job is not providing the happiness you thought it would. Then you try to

Be Bold (Step 2), and you are not sure what it is that you want. You are stuck. You are feeling anxious, or you are judging yourself for not being happy at a job that has such good benefits. Maybe you keep telling yourself that this is just life. No one is really happy, right? You've typed your starting destination into the travel search engine, but now you don't know where you want to fly to. You've finally admitted that "here" is not where you want to be, but you don't know where you want to go.

If you find yourself not knowing where to go or what step to take next, the most important thing you can ask yourself at that point is:

What am I afraid of?

Your first answers might be something like:

- *I'm afraid of not having an income.*
- *I'm afraid of not being able to pay my bills.*
- *I'm afraid that I'm stuck in this job because of my age or my education.*

And all of those things are probably true for you. But I'm going to suggest that you dig a little bit deeper and ask yourself, "What am I REALLY afraid of?" Maybe you can see that your real fear is that you don't want to become like your father. You saw him come home every night disgruntled and unhappy at his job. But he felt stuck because he placed providing for his family above his own happiness. Now, this is not wrong. However, you as a young child might have watched your father die slowly every day in a job that he hated. There is no way to shield that from a family. Your father made his choices in a different time and probably for different reasons than you are making your choices. Maybe your fear is that you are turning into your father. Your father died at age 55 of a heart attack, and you don't know that your father ever experienced happiness.

So you're thinking about your job, but your fear is that you'll never find happiness in your own life. You are afraid that you will follow the same path as your father and die never having truly found your dream. When you find yourself worrying or struggling, understand that you are not *Being Still.*

Worrying is you trying to solve the problem all by yourself,
without the power of God or the universe.

And what is the opposite of worry and fear? Faith. Faith in that power. Faith that the power is on your side and wants you to be happy and content. Whatever your worldview, can you really imagine that the power that created the universe wants to see you fail or wants to see you unhappy? Doesn't it make more sense that whatever being or power that created this world we live in and created us, created us for joy?

12

Step 4: Be Aware

Here's the fun part. You have accepted your current situation and you've been honest with your feelings about it. Then, you figured out where you wanted to go. You asked God or the universe to help you get what it is that you need. You let go of how that answer was going to come to you. You let go of your desire for a particular outcome or to have that outcome arrive at a particular time. Then, you were still. You have been waiting on God and the universe to provide you with what it is you really need. Now is the time to *Be Aware.*

Being Aware is looking around for the universe's response.

Help and response can come to you in a variety of ways. If you are listening to your intuition, it may come to you in a feeling. This is different than just a passing thought where you might continue to question the response. This is a knowing, deep down in your gut that you need to take that next step. If you pray, the answers may come to you in prayer. Messages can also come during meditations.

If you don't meditate or pray, the responses may come to you in a different way. There are signs from the universe around us every single day. You just have to look for them. And the more you look for them and the more you are open to seeing them, the more you will see. These signs and wonders can be sent to you as messages in a multitude of ways. The universe is not limited by anything. If you believe that God created the universe, then He is not going to be limited by anything else either.

There are a lot of books and information available about the meaning of signs and symbols. Sometimes, when I see a sign, I enjoy looking up the possible spiritual significance. Repeating numbers can be a sign that the universe sends. This can be a good one for people who aren't hearing their own intuition. If you start seeing the number 1 repeating on clocks, on billboards, in stores, on signs, this might be the universe sending you a message. These repeating numbers can be any number. They don't have to be the number 1.

The universe can also send you particular animals that cross your path or come into your presence. I have a lot of clients who get messages both through repeating numbers and through animals that keeping showing up for them. But don't be limited.

I, myself, have gotten many messages through television commercials. I think it's kind of funny that I get a deep spiritual insight from a fast food commercial. But it's happened more than once!

You may have a friend or family member contact you out of the blue. They could say something to you or give you feedback that is exactly the answer you were looking for. It might even be someone you talked to in the grocery store who says something to you that just seems to resonate. You are only limited here by your willingness to accept the messages.

A well-known psychologist, Carl Jung, coined the term "synchronicity," which describes a meaningful coincidence. We have all experienced them. Think about that person who called you out of the blue minutes after you were thinking about them. Or that check you got in the mail right at the time that you had a bill due and did not know how you were going to pay for it. It's those unexplained coincidences that have meaning. Those are the responses from the universe. If you are not looking for them or you are not open to seeing them, you will miss them. If your eyes are closed, you will probably find that you don't see these synchronicities. However, if you approach your day with your eyes open, expecting a response from God or the universe, then you will begin to see these answers everywhere you look.

Author Louise Hay has long made the connection between the body's messages and the emotional situations we are dealing with. I refer to her books when I have a particular health issue or pain to help me in understanding what emotional issue may need addressing. Looking at the emotional messages that your body may be sending you does not mean that you need to ignore the medical issue. If you have pain in your leg, for example, and you go to the doctor for treatment, you can also check in with what God or the universe is telling you about this particular pain in your body. You can do both at the same time.

There are an unlimited number of ways that the universe will speak to us. In Step 3, we were *Still* and allowed the universe to do its thing. Step 4: Be Aware, requires us to be aware of the answers that are being sent our way. Those responses can come through a gut feeling or a deep knowing in our hearts. The responses can also come in signs and wonders from the universe. The power in the universe is not limited. You only have to *Be Aware.*

13

All Four Steps Put Together

Let's take an example from start to finish so that you can see the four steps in action. I love this example, both because of its simplicity and because it quickly helped one of my clients with a big decision. She and her husband were considering moving to a different house. They have two young children. The house that they are currently living in is a good house, she likes it, and there really isn't anything wrong with it. Except for one major problem. The bedrooms are on two different levels. She and her husband sleep on a different level than their young children.

Recently, in a nearby neighborhood, new houses started being built and they were all single-story homes. This got their attention. They looked at some of the new homes and liked them. What's the problem, you ask? Well, making a decision to move is a big decision. The new houses were more expensive and they had an emotional attachment to the house they currently lived in.

This is when my client came to me. She really didn't know what to do. Should she stay or should she move? She told me that she had spent hours being conflicted about this choice. She had already toured the new houses a number of times. She had researched interest rates and mortgage calculators and started listing the pros and cons of staying versus moving. She also knew that her children were going to grow up and the bedrooms being on different floors wasn't always going to be a problem. In the end, she was struggling.

I told her about the four steps to an easier life. She laughed and said, "Sign me up!" I encouraged her to use the four steps and stop the struggling by getting direction from the universe instead of trying to figure it out for herself. She jumped right in and here's what happened.

Step 1: Be Open: This client was open about her feelings and her struggle in trying to decide whether or not to move. She could admit that she felt stuck. She also admitted that she was frustrated. She felt guilty because she didn't want her children to be upset or scared. She admitted her feelings and her struggle. She knew there was a reason, not only for her concern about her current home, but a reason that new homes were being built in her area. She was open to her current situation, allowed it to be what it was, and acknowledged her feelings about the situation.

Step 2: Be Bold: In this step, my client stated where she wanted to go. She wanted to get assistance and direction on whether or not she and her family should move. She was able to let go of holding on tightly to one outcome or another.

Her struggle had been that she kept using her own power and energy to try and solve a problem. And she was not getting where she wanted to go. Although she knew where she wanted to go, she was struggling with how to get there. This client was displaying a classic example of using all of her own power to try and figure out the right decision. It was taking a lot of energy. She didn't know what to do and she was continuing to struggle.

Step 3: Be Still: When *Being Still,* you need to stop continuing to pursue a particular outcome. In this example, she stopped looking at new houses. She stopped looking at the interest rate fluctuations, and she stopped looking at her budget. She put away her list of pros and cons.

This is why this step can be difficult for people who like to be in control of all of their decisions. This client is generally like that, but she was also able to see the futility in continuing to make lists and research options. She had been doing that for months.

She needed help with making the best choice for her family. At this point, her role was to let all of that go. The work was done. She had asked the universe for help, and now she needed to let the universe supply her with the answer. If she continued trying to figure out what to do, then she would not have been letting go of the problem, and she would have continued to struggle.

Step 4: Be Aware: Before she and her husband applied this system, they had already spoken with a lender. They wanted a good idea of how to budget and what price house they could really afford. *Being Still* doesn't mean that you are doing nothing. It means that you are no longer trying to solve the problem by yourself. You've asked a power greater than you to create the solution.

Not long after applying these steps, my client and her husband heard back from the lender. They got news that they were not expecting. Their application was denied. Both she and her husband worked and had good jobs. It seems that there was a problem with a rental property they owned. I don't know the details. However, it was affecting their credit, and my client and her husband had not realized this. Even though they had sufficient income, this particular bank said that they would not give them a loan.

My client was actually pretty excited when she talked to me about this. She said that normally she and her husband would have gone to a different bank or continued to push for their own solution. But because they had let go of being invested in any particular outcome, they believed that this response from the bank was the sign they had asked for.

They had asked the universe to help, and the universe responded. It was now time to listen to that response. As a result, they did not try to get a loan from anyone else. This client tells me how much she felt at peace throughout this whole process. She knew, instinctively, that being denied the loan was the universe telling her not to move. Because she wasn't invested in one particular outcome, she was totally okay with that direction.

This entire process, the four steps, took her just a few days from start to finish. She tells me of how much time and how much energy she and her husband had put into deciding whether or not to move. Once they applied this system, the struggle stopped. The worry stopped. They had the answer they needed.

This example is very straightforward. It was both simple and complex at the same time. My client used the system and put it into effect in just a few days. That's the simple part. And she was deciding whether or not to buy a new home. That's the complex part.

When does this program go from helping with straightforward decisions to helping with your life? **It happens when you accept that your current situation has a purpose and you have confidence and faith that God or the universe is taking care of you.** You can then let go of taking control and allow that power that is greater than you to continue taking care of you. Then this program goes from one of just simple decision making to one that can change your life.

Now let's consider an example where the four steps were being used, but not in their entirety. Last year, early one morning, I turned on my coffee maker and nothing happened. If you knew me, you would know that I don't want to go one day without coffee. So, I set out to buy a new coffee maker right away. I went to the store, and with the intention of using this four-step system. I asked God to show me which coffee maker to get.

A few years ago, I would have spent hours doing research on what coffee maker had the best customer feedback and provided all the features I was looking for. But not this day. I marched right into the store without any research or thought at all and walked directly to the kitchen department. I saw the same coffee maker that I had been using and I thought, "This will be easy." I liked my old drip coffee maker. However, this store did not have any available. They had a display of my particular model but did not have it in stock.

I then thought about buying one of those coffee makers where you use the little coffee pods that make one cup at a time. Most people I know had them and I had considered buying one in the past, but never had.

I went around the corner and looked at the other type of coffee makers. Then I got frustrated. I couldn't tell the difference between three or four of the different versions of that same coffee maker. There was a sign that showed what features each of them had. The problem was that the sign did not match up with any of the versions this store was selling. I read each of the four boxes. I looked at the tags on the display models. But I was still not any closer to understanding what it was they were selling.

All I had wanted to do was walk into a store and buy a simple coffee maker. Yet, here I was getting upset because the one item I wanted was not available and the other item that sounded good was really just confusing me. I didn't know if I should go to a different store, walk to the front and find someone to help me (it was a big store and very busy, so this could have been difficult), or just leave and try to live a caffeine-free life.

I took a deep breath and reminded myself that I have a great system that works in situations exactly like this. I did not need to be getting upset about this purchase. I set about using this four-step system. Here's what it looked like:

1. **Be Open:** I admitted to myself that I was frustrated about the added task in a busy week. It bothered me that such a simple purchase had gotten so confusing and time-consuming. I also was angry that I couldn't

seem to find anyone to help me. I was not very accepting of this situation.

2. **Be Bold:** I asked God for direction on which coffee maker to buy.
3. **Be Still:** I took a few deep breaths and tried to let go of the tension. I stopped comparing one product to another. I also went back to look at the original drip coffee makers.
4. **Be Aware:** I started looking for feedback from the universe. After double-checking that the original coffee maker was not available, I left that section. Then I went back to the section that had the single-pod coffee makers. I was still a little frustrated, but I was also looking around for the answer to my problem.

Just then, a store clerk came over and asked if I needed help. I explained to her that I was having a hard time understanding the difference in the four products and I was confused that the guide on the shelf did not seem to correspond to any of the coffee makers I was looking at. The clerk ended up being very helpful, including agreeing with me that their display was quite confusing.

I have a very specific purpose in telling you this story. I did a number of things wrong, and I think it would be helpful to point them out. I started out being a little cranky. This was because of reasons other than needing a new coffee maker. However, I was not expecting the help or allowing the process to be easy. I was not open to my initial situation. That was my first mistake.

I walked into the store asking God for direction on which coffee maker to buy. I went right to the one that I thought I was going to buy and then found out it was out of stock. I had asked for direction and then I didn't follow that direction. That was mistake number two.

My third mistake was being attached to a particular outcome. When I looked back on my own process, I realized that I had asked for direction and had walked right to the coffee maker that I wanted and the outcome I wanted. When the feedback was that the outcome would be different than I had originally thought, I became disappointed and frustrated. That means I was only willing to allow the one outcome that I wanted. If I had gone into the store *Being Open* to any option, then a specific coffee maker that was not available should not have disappointed me. After all, I had given the decision over to the universe.

Do I think that God talks to us through poorly-stocked shelves? Yes, I do.

But it's okay if you don't. My biggest error was that I was not allowing it to be easy. My frustration and my irritability were of my own doing. Even if I did not believe that the first coffee pot being out of stock was a response from the universe, I was still holding on to one particular outcome. Then I became disappointed when I did not get exactly what I was expecting.

I provided this example, not only to show that this process can be used even for the very simple choices we make in life as well as the big ones, but also to show where we can make the process more difficult than it is. I did end up with a great coffee maker that I love. However, that 45-minute shopping trip did not have to be difficult at all. I could have made it very easy. I got stuck along the way. I was still able to turn things around and make it work. Now when I'm sipping coffee in the morning, I wonder why I waited so long to get a fancy coffee maker!

Have you ever found yourself saying, **"I'm trying really hard and I just can't get what I want."**

Understand the two errors in this approach:

1. "I'm trying" – Change that to "I'm allowing" the situation to unfold as it is supposed to. When you are relying solely on your own power, you are not connecting with the power in the universe.
2. I can't get what "I want" – It is easy to focus on a particular outcome and to hold tightly to your way being the only acceptable outcome. However, letting go of how the solution or direction will be provided for you allows for an abundance of options.

14

Where to Go From Here

This four-step system is easy to learn. It is a bit more complex to implement into your life. Why is that? The system works. Most of you will not have difficulty in understanding what each step is about. The reason why it's a little harder to implement these steps is because of a word that therapists like to call "resistance."

All behavior that we engage in serves a purpose. If it wasn't working for us on some level, we wouldn't do it. If eating that piece of chocolate cake did nothing for you, you would have no problem avoiding it. But not only does it taste really good, it also elevates the endorphins and other hormones in our body that allow us to feel good. Even though you know that eating chocolate cake every single day may not be that beneficial to your health, you still indulge sometimes. It's serving a purpose.

You may also have another purpose, like wanting to lose weight. You can allow that bigger purpose to

ABOUT THE AUTHOR

Michell Torres is a psychotherapist who has practiced in California for over 25 years. Upon obtaining her license to practice psychotherapy, she began doing psychiatric crisis interventions at hospital emergency departments. Her role included evaluating patients who came into the emergency department or were admitted to the hospital with psychiatric emergencies. Within two years, she became the manager of that program and spent the next 15 years managing the 24/7 psychiatric crisis program at two different trauma centers. She has also owned a private practice for nearly 20 years.

A few years ago, realizing that she was not satisfied with the course her life was taking, she faced the decision to continue working as a manager in the hospital or to start her own business.

At first, she approached it very practically. But soon determined that although she had done all the logical steps, she still didn't know which choice was the right one for her. Out of that struggle, came this program.

Since leaving the hospital job, she continues her private practice and is now an integrative health practitioner, an author, and consultant.